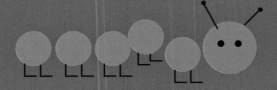

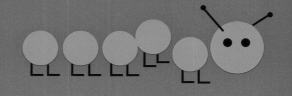

**Andrews McMeel
Publishing**

Kansas City

THIS BOOK IS FOR ALL KIDS, BUT especially MY SISTER LIBBY.

LIBBY DIED.

BY JACK SIMON, WHEN HE WAS 5 YEARS OLD.
ILLUSTRATED BY HIS MOM, annette SIMON,
WHEN SHE WAS 36 YEARS OLD.

This Book Is for All Kids, but Especially My Sister Libby. Libby Died. Copyright © 2002 by Jack and Annette Simon. All rights reserved. Printed in China. No part of this book may be used or reproduced in any manner whatsoever without written permission except in the case of reprints in the context of reviews. For information, write Andrews McMeel Publishing, an Andrews McMeel Universal company, 4520 Main Street, Kansas City, Missouri 64111.

02 03 04 05 06 WKT 10 9 8 7 6 5 4 3 2 1

ISBN: 0-7407-2952-7

Library of Congress Control Number: 2002105012

Mighty Max® is a trademark owned by Mattel, Inc., used with permission.

─────── ATTENTION: SCHOOLS AND BUSINESSES ───────

Andrews McMeel books are available at quantity discounts with bulk purchase for educational, business, or sales promotional use. For information, please write to: Special Sales Department, Andrews McMeel Publishing, 4520 Main Street, Kansas City, Missouri 64111.

THIS BOOK IS FOR ALL KIDS, BUT especially my SISTER LIBBY.

LIBBY DIED.

THIS BOOK IS FOR ALL KIDS, BUT ESPECIALLY MY SISTER LIBBY.

LIBBY DIED.

for our moms and dads.
for Kent. for Grant.
for all our family, especially Libby.
—Jack & Annette

DID YOU

HEAR me?

SHE DIED.

and when you
even have to (

DIE, YOU DON'T
T CHICKEN POX.

ve FOOD. YOU DON'T even need FOOD.

I'M HUNGRY.

LIBBY WAS JUST SO SICK, NO DOCTORS COULD HELP H

SHE'S TH

mom,

WHAT IF LIBBY WAS YOUR FIRST BABY, AND I WAS THE MIDDLE K

SO SHE HAD TO DIE.

SO SHE DID.

SHE'S THE FIRST ONE IN OUR FAMILY TO DIE.
RST ONE TO BE WITH THE ANGELS.

WOULD IT HAVE BEEN ME?   WOULD I BE DEAD NOW?

WELL, WHEN
JUST PUT MY
SUPERHERO
FIGURES ON
SO I CAN BR
UP TO heaven
and we can
WITH THEM

Maybe someo

I DIE,

ACTION
MY CHEST
IG THEM
WITH ME
PLAY

Yeah, if i could ask libby about being in heaven

You're dea

and how do an

wings out of th

do you move th

with wing insti

wouldn't it be funny if you had wings coming o

O HOW EXACTLY DO YOU LIVE?

LS GROW THOSE
IR BACKS? HOW
n? DO THEY COME
JCTIONS?

YOUR EYEBALLS? OR ON YOUR BUTT? hahahaha

and if you don't need your body anymor

e THERE JUST HEADS FLOATING AROUND?

mom, WILL LIBBY HaVE THE same fa

WILL we have

HOW WILL we ReCOGNIZ

D CLOTHES ON WHEN WE SEE HER AS AN ANGEL?

ALL THE ANGELS WHICH ONES ARE NAMED LIBBY?

ER?

DO ANGELS
SLEEP? DO

STAY AWAKE

AND EVERY

EVER GO TO

THEY

EVERY DAY

NIGHT?

I WOULD LIKE TO ASK HE

LIKE HOW MUCH DOES SH

a sad question, too…

ove us and miss us.

HEY, LIBBY ... DID YOU GET THE BALLOONS

ew UP FOR YOUR BIRTHDAY?

in Hea

are you

as you

on ea

en,
as BIG
were
TH?

WOW.

now you know what god looks like.

WHEN YOU DIE, YOU ca

and DOORS and

even LIBBY. WHEN she wa

mixed up. SHE couldn'

CRaWL anyWHeRe, BU

F   L   o   a   T

FLOAT THROUGH WALLS

TUFF THAT YOU CAN'T DO NOW.

ALIVE, HER BONES WERE

EVEN HUG ANYONE OR

HOW SHE CAN EVEN

THROUGH WALLS.

I KNOW! IT'S LIKE ALADDIN'S GENIE.

WHEN YOU'RE ON EARTH, YOUR BODY'S LIKE YOUR MAST

AND WHEN YOU DIE, YOU'RE SE

F

R   e   e.

RIGHT, LII

and since you can now...

GIVE GOD A HUG FOR ME, TOO.

BY!

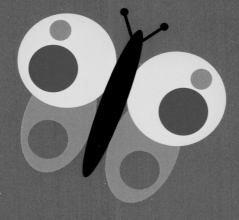